ENGLISH COSTUME OF THE
SEVENTEENTH CENTURY

English Costume
of the
Seventeenth Century

Drawn and Described by
IRIS BROOKE

Adam & Charles Black

FIRST PUBLISHED 1934
REPRINTED 1947
SECOND EDITION 1950
REPRINTED 1958, 1964, 1971, 1977
© A & C BLACK LTD
35 BEDFORD ROW, LONDON WC1R 4JH
ISBN 0 7136 0157 4

REPRODUCED BY COLOURCRAFTSMEN LTD
PRINTED IN GREAT BRITAIN BY TINDAL PRESS
CHELMSFORD, ESSEX

FOREWORD

ALTHOUGH the aim and scope of the books in this series are self-evident to most readers, it seems desirable to touch on two points in this connection. In the first place, they are not intended for, nor would they interest, those who have made a life-study of historic costume and who are primarily concerned with the intricacies of the subject. My purpose is to provide a useful guide and not a serious text-book, to give elementary descriptions of costume for those who have neither time nor inclination to pore over countless prints, paintings, and actual examples, yet who wish to obtain a comprehensive idea of the dress of the period. The condensation of any aspect of a whole century into less than one hundred pages necessitates so high a degree of selection that many of its omissions and inclusions equally are open to debate. Nevertheless, to those with slight knowledge of the subject, wishing to select costumes from a certain decade in history, a book of this size is infinitely more useful than a tome fifty times its weight and extent, which would certainly give more detail but probably fewer actual examples of the complete costume desired.

Secondly, it is clear that detail cannot be dealt with beyond a certain measure of accuracy in full-length drawings of three or four inches high when the figure from which the costume is taken is usually life-size and sometimes larger. A minute study of such details as collars, belts, shoes, gloves, and dozens of other equally interesting items can be made satisfactorily only in the excellent collections of the articles themselves, such as are found, for example, in several of the museums in and around London.

The Stuart period is perhaps the most romantic in English

history, a period in which men duelled and danced, fought hard and loved hard, with equal grace and accomplishment, in satins and lace. There was brutality enough and bitter feeling in the seventeenth century, war and suffering in abundance ; yet contemporary portraiture has preserved a remarkable appearance of unruffled exquisiteness. These ghosts in wigs and ribbons, satins and silks, seem to live on more vividly than the historic facts with which they are surrounded—the Civil Wars of Cavalier and Roundhead, the Great Plague, the Fire of London, Monmouth's Rebellion, and the infamies of Judge Jeffreys. Memorable as these events were, those who took part in them, unrivalled in history in their apparently haughty indifference to plagues, fires, wars, and massacres, have left a more enduring impression, an impression of gay bravado reflected in and emphasized by their extravagance in clothes.

I. B.

1600—1610

SO little change is remarkable during the first ten years of the seventeenth century, that it will be unnecessary to dwell upon each portion of the fashionable garments in detail. The century opens with the flamboyant and ungainly clothing of Elizabeth's Court. Stiff, bombasted, and doll-like, these figures in ruffles, farthingales, exaggerated breeches, and quilted garments leave a lasting picture on one's mind.

Anne of Denmark, the new Queen, has long been famed for her complete lack of taste in clothes, and in her hands rested the reformation, or otherwise, of the existing fashions. Unfortunately, her fancy led her to encourage and exaggerate the already hideous and deforming costumes then prevalent at Court. History informs us that on the death of Elizabeth, her ladies proceeded to Berwick, to greet James I's queen, laden with the jewels and gowns of their late-lamented queen. If we are to believe the reputed size of the virgin Queen's wardrobe, it is not inconceivable that Anne should have converted a few hundred, at least, of these costly and regal gowns to her own use. If this were the case, it might possibly explain the seeming lack of progress in fashion during the ensuing fifteen years !

The farthingale—ugliest of all modes—continued in fashion and increased in size, in spite of the King's bad-tempered endeavour to exterminate it, until the death of Anne in 1619. It appears that at a grand masque at Court, several of the ladies became wedged in the passage, and so completely blocked the entrance, that half or more of the guests never managed to get into the hall or attend the masque. After this tiresome experience, James issued a proclamation forbidding the farthingale to be worn at Court ("This impertinent garment takes up all the room at Court") either by ladies or gentlemen—for the gallants not to be outdone by the fairer sex padded their breeches to a corresponding extent. No notice, however, was taken of this order, for the simple reason that the Queen flatly refused to abandon her favourite form of dress.

1600—1610 (*continued*)

Such fabulous sums were expended abroad on materials—silks, satins, velvets, etc., that one or two spirited endeavours were made to promote interest in the manufacture of materials at home. Mulberry farms were started in several parts of the country and silk-worms imported. Silk-growing survived for nearly a hundred years, and was only abandoned when the futility of protecting the mulberry trees in the chilly winter months was realized.

In the year 1599, William Lee, Master of Arts, at St. John's College, Cambridge, devised an " engine " or steel loom for knitting or weaving silk stockings, waistcoats, etc. From that date there were few ladies or gentlemen who denied themselves the luxury, comfort, and extravagance of silk stockings, even at £2 to £5 per pair.

The large sums paid for clothes seem out of all proportion to the salaries and incomes of the time. A plush cloak might cost £50; plush being sold at the ghastly price of £3. 10s. per yard (and exceedingly narrow it was, too); and of course, no garment was considered fit for a gentleman unless embroidered or guarded with lace or velvet. The importance of appearance may be seen in Ben Jonson's *Magnetic Lady* : " . . . He has stained my new white satin doublet and bespattered my spic and span silk stockings on the day they were drawn on, and here's a spot in my hose too "—this after a vulgar brawl.

Trimmings played just as important a part as they had during the sixteenth century ; lace, ribbons, embroidery, artificial flowers, enamel, and jewels of all kinds, even coloured and gilded leather-work, were still placed indiscriminately on every garment—male or female. The Queen had a murrey-coloured satin gown ornamented with gilded cut leather sent her as a gift from the Queen of Spain. Breast-plates and collars of enamel and silver, or other fine metals, swords with embroidered and jewelled scabbards and sheaths, were frequently worn by men as part of their civil dress. Embroidered gloves, handsomely trimmed with fringe and tassels, were as necessary to the would-be élite as the embroidered and rosetted shoes.

1600—1610 (*continued*)

Long, loose gowns reaching to the ground, and trimmed with "shagg"—a long fur-like plush—or real fur, or even velvet, were worn by elderly gentlemen, or within the comparative privacy of one's own family circle. These gowns had the loose split sleeve, hanging from the shoulder, which formed the chief place of ornamentation. The breeches with canions, worn by the gentleman on the top right hand of the page facing, are composed entirely of heavy braid about an inch and a half to two inches wide—interlaced and sewn so as to leave a space through which a contrasting lining may be seen. With this form of nethergarment the stockings are tied just below the knees, and often hanging over the garter like the tops of boots. Overstockings, with leather soles and embroidered tops ; separate stocking-tops and boot-hose, were all worn at this period, and boots with coloured linings made of soft fancy leather were sometimes worn. It was not until the 'twenties, however, that the fashion was carried to an extreme. The large skirt-like breeches tended to elongate, giving them a squarish line at the knee, instead of the barrel shape of the earlier type ; to bring the latter more up to date, tassels and ribbons were frequently attached at the knee.

A kind of slipper, similar to a mule, with a heel about an inch or more in height, was worn to a considerable extent within doors. Doublets and bodices of embroidered linen were worn by both sexes, and often caps or bonnets of similar design, and edged with lace, were made to match. There is an example of a lady wearing one of the caps at the bottom of the opposite page ; and on the following page may be seen a gentleman in his indoor cap.

1600—1610 (*continued*)

Many and varied were the types of collar worn during this period—from the large Elizabethan ruffle to the flat lace collar worn by the little girl at the bottom of the second page of illustrations to this decade. A sufficiently comprehensive selection may be seen on these four pages.

In the year 1604 " James I by letter patents did incorporate the felt-makers of London, by the name of Hatter & Warders or Mistery of Feltmakers of London granting them divers privileges and liberties." Another endeavour to support home industries and thereby cut out the importation of Spanish and French beavers and felts ! Men's hats were overwhelmingly large and covered in feathers and jewels— and correspondingly expensive ! In Ben Jonson's *The Devil is an Ass*, the prize for a wager takes the form of " A new Four pound beaver hat, set with enamel studs." Any coloured hat was fashionable, although greys and blacks seemed most popular.

The hair-dressing or head-tiring of the ladies shows little or no difference from that of ten or even twenty-five years earlier. Quantities of jewellery was still worn in the hair, and saffron hair-dye remained a favourite tint. The black velvet hat with plumes of feathers still perched at an absurd angle on the back of the head, and any odd jewel or trinket that had not found a resting-place in my lady's periwig might be placed with impunity upon her hat !

1610—1620

ON the opposite page may be seen two excellent examples of the costumes of this period—the lady's
taken from one of Anne's numerous portraits, and the other
from a portrait of Henry, Prince of Wales. The extraordinary stiffness and impracticability of these clothes may
be easily seen from these figures. It will be noticed that
the bombasted breeches of the boy are split at the knee
showing the lining—a fashion that became extremely
prevalent during the twenties and 'thirties. The lined
boots and boot-hose are also exceedingly advanced—as
more of them are to be seen at a later date. The blue collar
is an interesting point worthy of note, as, previously, collars
had mostly been made of lawn, holland, or some white
or natural-coloured material. The passion for decorating
garments with gold braid or metal ribbon may be observed.
Plain, indeed, was the doublet of this period if it were not
ornamented with several yards of lace, embroidery, leather,
bead-work, or braid. This suit was, in all probability, made
of plush, of somewhat similar texture to the panne velvet of
to-day.

This farthingale, similar to those worn by Elizabeth, was
probably made according to the fashionable lady's require-
ments. " High at the back and low in the front, the sides
wide, that I may rest my arms upon it." The collar was
wired to keep it at the necessary angle to make a charming
background to a well-painted picture !

Many hours' patient work were expended on my lady's
toilet, many layers of clothes had to be fitted and fixed, and
cosmetics had not yet arrived at any degree of perfection.
The Spanish " papers " for rouge and powder did not arrive
in England until many years later. A bag of chalk served
the purpose of our modern powder-box !

1610—1620 (*continued*)

The last figure on this page has been specially inserted to show the arrangement of the skirt. To obtain the required outline, giant sausage-shaped horse-shoes of hair or rags were tied over the petticoat below the waist—the gown then being allowed to fall over this unwholesome piece of absurdity. This would account for the gown always being split up the front when the farthingale was worn, to facilitate the tying and arranging of the padding necessary to obtain the fashionable silhouette.

Ladies' hunting-suits or riding-habits of the day were not designed with the idea of giving any comfort to their wearers ; it was not even unusual to ride in a farthingale. If we are to take the portraits of the queen as typical of a fashionable lady's habit, we may perceive her dressed in a low revealing doublet, with stiff wired collar encircling the back of her head and neck, and making any neck movement difficult if not impossible. Full-padded sleeves split in the demands of fashion to expose the smock ; her skirts, if not actually concealing the farthingale—full-padded and trailing. An absurd hat of grey beaver, with a ridiculously high crown ornamented with feathers and enamel studs, perched unsafely on the front of her piled up hair.

The costume of the masked lady on the opposite page is also taken from a contemporary print of a group of ladies riding—although here the farthingale is small. It is difficult to imagine that a riding-suit of this sort could ever have been coped with, or worn with any degree of comfort. It will be noticed here that the lady is wearing a band under the chin—a device which appears to have accompanied the mask in various forms throughout the century. This particular mask was known as a Loo or half-mask.

Cuffs increased considerably during the decade, sometimes even being made in layers of three or four, and reaching above the elbow.

1610—1620 *(continued)*

An interesting variation of the immense breeches of the period may be observed at the top of the opposite page ; these were cut on the lines of the open-breeches introduced some ten or fifteen years earlier, the gathering round the waist and the tightening of the hem giving a curious barrel effect. The doublet, too, is interesting in this example, as it shows a definite tendency to pad at the chest instead of having, as previously, all the padding near the belt. This latter fashion having survived in a much moderated form ever since the introduction of the Peas-cod doublet of the previous century.

After the death of Anne of Denmark, the ladies, having no leader to spur them on to further exaggerations and extravagances and no Court to dazzle with their magnificence, assumed a more subdued version of the previous fashions, and no longer vied with each other to wear the largest and most cumbersome petticoats, or the tallest head of hair most filled with jewels. And although one cannot, with any stretch of imagination, say that simplicity was the vogue, yet, after the extraordinarily bizarre and ostentatious fashions of the last quarter of a century, these ladies must have appeared amazingly subdued to one brought up in the wealthiest period of English History, and accustomed to the overdressed and over-bejewelled ladies and gentlemen at the Court of Good Queen Bess and the flamboyant Anne of Denmark.

From now onwards and until well into the eighteenth century the fairer sex held no light to the gallants in the matter of clothes. Every man had a thousand opportunities of adding a ribbon, a jewel, a fringe, a piece of lace, braid, rosette or curl ; of showing an embroidered stocking, stocking-tips, costly boots, garters, and so on ; whilst the woman must content herself with lace collars and cuffs, and perhaps a bunch of ribbons here or there.

1610—1620 (*continued*)

Beards and moustaches continued in favour until the 'eighties, and an amusing example of a beard, looking suspiciously artificial may be seen in the middle of the opposite page. The curly type of beard running round the chin to the jaw bones was most prevalent. This might be worn as in the picture of the man at the top of the page, or clipped to a point like that of the man at the bottom of the previous page. Men's hats had by now reached the height of their decoration—and price ! Enamel studs and jewels of every kind found their place in the expensive hat-bands of the élite ; and large metal or gold clasps, with coloured stones, were used to fix the feather decoration securely to the hat itself. So valuable were these hats that they were the first item to be removed by a highway thief or footpad. Men were lured within doors and their hats snatched before they had any idea who their assailant might be.

Gigantic pear-shaped pearls and stars, arrows, crescents, etc., were made in enamel and set with stones to wear in the hair. Pearls were so much worn at this time that even the edge of a collar might be closely set with these precious stones. The charming little lace-caps, already described, were not worn in England later than about 1618 or 1620. Caps were discarded for half a century or more in favour of a more elegant and informal type of hair-dressing. One notices that wherever the cap was worn in previous times the hair seemed to suffer in consequence. Few curls were allowed to escape from their hiding-place beneath layers of lace. Possibly the caps in history were invented for the busy woman who had no time for decorative hair-dressing, and just bundled up her hair beneath a cap, jammed on to hide any deficiencies.

1620—1630

THE first period of this decade was singularly lacking in advancement—or indeed any style at all. When the Queen died, James, devoid of feminine influence, had the Court cleared of women, and abandoned himself to drink and vice. The royal children had already been placed in the charge of various noblewomen about the country. The Court became a scene of carousing and debauchery, and fashions in England practically remained at a standstill. A few new modes filtered across the Channel, but until the vivacious and witty young Henrietta Maria arrived, bringing with her a Parisienne trousseau, the country had no one to lead them in fashions.

From the arrival on these shores in June 1625 of the daughter of France, a revolution in ladies' dress commenced. Gone were the farthingales, ruffles, and long stomachers. High short-waisted bodices with Medici collars, low revealing corsages, and soft silk petticoats reaching to the ground replaced the stiff brocaded, cheese-like short petticoats.

I have selected the garments on the opposite page—not because they are significant of 1620—but because they show a definite link between the new fashion and the old. The exact date of the woman's dress is probably about 1628, and the man's 1624. With the latter may be seen a shortening of the doublet together with an elongation of the "skirts" or "tassets"—the ruffle in its last form—breeches changing from the short "trunks" into knee-breeches with an ornamented hem.

The lady's dress still holds something of the stiffness of Elizabethan times—the long stomacher is there, but the new high waist-line is emphasized by a ribbon tied under the arm-pits. The petticoat is short—while the gown assumes the new length touching the ground. The hair is dressed in a definitely transitional stage; it is still crimped and drawn back from the forehead, but a tiny fringe is visible, and a few small curls are allowed to hang over the ears, which for several years had been displayed. Later it will be noticed the fringe developed into a row of neat curls, and the side-curls became more and more exaggerated until the 'nineties.

1620—1630 (continued)

Few of the drawings on these four pages represent clothes worn earlier than 1625, as the advancement between 1618 and 1625 was so slight. With Charles I comes a difference. Before the stereotyped dress associated with this unhappy king became prevalent, for a few years there was a slightly experimental stage. Doublets were many and varied in design; some in the French style with the square-cut skirts, so beautifully illustrated by Abraham Bosse, were introduced in about 1628. The leather jerkin, sleeveless and reaching half-way down the thigh, was worn by civilians as well as by the Militia of that time. These continued in favour until well into the 'sixties; sometimes they were devoid of decoration—sometimes fringed and ornamented at the hem and arm-holes.

Leg-wear by about 1627 or 1629 had taken the form of loose knee-breeches, tied or sewn down the side to within five or six inches of the knee, and from there to the garter gaping open to show the fine lining. An example of this may be seen on the top right-hand figure on the opposite page. Some of the breeches had fringe or lace at the knee, and often stockings with decorated stocking-tops were tied just below the knee, giving the same effect as an edge. These stocking-tops were worn over the ordinary stockings; the habit of wearing two or more pairs seems prevalent from about 1625 until the end of the century.

Boots and boot-hose increased in size and decoration—the bucket-topped boot becoming a necessary part of every would-be gallant's attire. Large flaps of a butterfly shape were worn over the instep of these monstrosities. Several contemporary satirists depict the fop straddling along in a ludicrous and ungainly walk impeded and finally tripped up by his enormous boots. Bows of ribbon and gigantic rosettes decorated the square, elongated toes of their shoes.

The rather attractive fashion of tucking up the petticoats was started towards the end of this decade—probably when the longer gowns were introduced and the ladies had some difficulty in negotiating the notoriously filthy streets without ruining their fine garments. At first the gowns were held up by hand, but later they were pinned or tied in a variety of fashions. The high-waisted, tabbed bodice diminished in length as it increased in width—the increased size of the sleeves and wide, pointed collars adding several inches to the shoulders of their wearers.

1 6 2 0—1 6 3 0 *(continued)*

Ladies' sleeves were often composed of three separate materials. First the sleeve of the " smock," or shift, of some fine holland or silk, and over this a multitude of ribbons reaching from shoulder to wrist tied below the elbow and revealing the lining as the ribbons fell from the arm. Over this ribbon was the short elbow-length sleeve belonging to the bodice or gown. This was cut to the epaulet on the shoulder in front and tied at the elbow, frequently reaching only across the back of the arm—as shown in the example at the top of the opposite page. The full sleeve was still worn a great deal, and there are a few examples before the 'thirties of a three-quarter length sleeve —as will be seen at the bottom of the opposite page. This style, however, did not become the rage until five or six years later.

On the previous page will be seen a girl in the peasant costume of the day. As this type of dress was worn for several years by the working-class, it will be unnecessary to frequently repeat it.

The period of lace had begun—lace cuffs, lace collars, lace at the wrist and knees, lace on gloves and stockings, lace even on hats, and every fine garment was "laced." Where previously a tiny edge of lace had been, a deep border took its place. Right through the century and well into the eighteenth the most beautiful and exquisite lace played an important part in the decoration of clothes.

1620—1630 (*continued*)

Veils became fashionable towards the end of the 'twenties. They were worn without a hat and consisted of a square piece of net laid over the head and reaching about as far as the mouth, the border often of lace.   One of these is illustrated in the next group of heads (1630–1640).   Hairdressing became more and more informal—the effect of nonchalance in the arrangement of the curls was belied by the neatness of the back-view.   At first the hair was puffed at the sides, giving an effect of short hair from the front; later, the front curls were cut shorter, or added, in cases where nature had not been sufficiently generous for the demands of fashion. From this time onwards until the introduction of the pinner or commode in the late 'seventies, fashionable ladies wore no hats or head-dresses, with the exception of hoods, that were not equally suitable for men.   The large beavers and felts, and even velvet caps, were exact replicas of their husband's or brother's.

Feathers decorated practically every hat.   Long curling plumes of ostrich feathers stuck out from the hat-bands and drooped over the shoulders of the gallants, mingling with their locks, now worn long.   The shoulder-length curls were now allowed to grow several inches over the collar. Some of the older men still adhered to the mode of short hair, but men of all ages wore the fashionable Van Dyck beard and moustaches, the brighter sparks curling their moustaches to ridiculous extremes, and clipping their beards to a sharp point.

The ruffle, having quite disappeared by 1627, was supplanted by the now famous Van Dyck collar.   Made of the most exquisite lace, they reached from the throat to points over the shoulders.   The stiffened pleated Medici collar remained in favour until the 'fifties.

1630—1640

THE cut of the doublet on the opposite page is typical of the 'thirties. Often the front was slashed in two or three places to show the shirt. The breeches were tied to the doublet at this time, with points threaded through the eyelet holes round the waist above the tabs or tassets. The epaulet was still worn on the shoulders of every doublet. Sleeves varied only slightly, all being formed of ribbons reaching from shoulder to wrist. Sometimes they were joined just below the elbow, and the forearm in this case was tightly fitting, but usually they hung loosely, showing large puffs of silk shirt. Cuffs were all made of lace or embroidered linen. The collar was edged with fine lace ; in this instance it is supported round the face, although this type of collar was rarely seen after 1630, the popularity of the Van Dyck collar sweeping other modes before it.

Children of either sex wore these charming little caps until they were four or five years old, little girls wearing them until they were eight or ten years of age. The pinafore or apron, decorated with fine lace, was worn by little girls throughout the entire century.

The embroidered bodice of the lady is very similar in design to that of her spouse—the same type of sleeve being equally fashionable for either sex. The ladies' costumes at this period were very subdued in contrast to those worn ten or twenty years earlier. Plain materials were more to be seen than patterned, and a lace collar and cuffs were often the only form of adornment.

The Queen was not extravagant in clothes, the duties of a mother claiming all her attention. In one of her letters she writes to France asking for a new petticoat-bodice, as she has nothing but a velvet one which she had two years previously, and that is worn and too short and tight to be fashionable. This modest request stands out in history after the ridiculous quantities of garments the two previous queens had indulged in. Of all the accusations hurled at this unhappy Queen, nothing could be said about her personal extravagance. The only other mention of wearing apparel in Henrietta Maria's letters seems to have been a request for one dozen pairs of sweet chamois gloves and one of doeskin.

1630--1640 (*continued*)

By 1630 all signs of padding and stuffing in the breeches had disappeared. They now hung loosely, fitting the leg to the knee, where they were usually tied with a lengthy and wide garter wound several times round the leg, and then tied in a large bow or arranged as a rosette. Boots continued in size and decorativeness and were rarely worn without the boot-hose, or stocking-tops, hanging over the turned-down top. The figure of the small boy at the top of the page is taken from a portrait of William of Orange, and it is interesting to note that as early as '39, the short coat was worn in the Netherlands, when it did not become prevalent in England until the 'forties. This example has the sleeves and slashing of the 'thirties, also the collar.

Ladies' hair was worn longer than previously, " heart-breakers," or long curls, being arranged to fall over the shoulders. Hair ornaments of pearls and ribbon were worn a great deal at either side of the " bun " at the back, and showing from the front. Little girls wore, what would to-day be called hair-ribbons, to tie their curls back from their forehead—as may be seen at the top of the opposite page.

The stomacher was nearly always cut in a U shape below the waist. The neck-line of the bodice no longer formed a V in front, a square being much more fashionable. This was usually very low cut, and often a tiny frill of lace protruded from the top of the bodice. Long strings of pearls were exceedingly fashionable, often being worn to emphasize the waist-line, and tied in a variety of fashions at the neck and waist.

Cuffs might fall softly from the three-quarter length sleeve or they might turn back, their " raggs " or points reaching to the elbow. Furs, stoles, or tippets were worn during the 'thirties; and the first umbrella appeared in England in this decade.

1630—1640 *(continued)*

So many are the brilliant drawings of Abraham Bosse, the son of a French tailor, and Wenceslaus Hollar during this period, that it is extremely difficult to make a selection of typical garments from the vast quantities available. The French and English styles differ a little, but as both must have been worn in England—Henrietta Maria never forgetting unfortunately that she was a Frenchwoman—both styles must be represented. The muff tied in the centre with ribbon, and the box-pleated petticoat are both amusing and unexpected. The mock-sleeves on the little child's gown are unusual at so advanced a period of the seventeenth century.

Capes, from the 'thirties onwards, were an indispensable part of every man's attire, and they were worn *under* the collar of the doublet. Hats became larger and with higher crowns as the 'forties approached. The French method of men's hairdressing consisted of a fuzzy bush of untidy curls around the face and head with several long curls hanging down the back ; whilst in England the more favourite method of dressing the hair was in a long curly " bob," resting on the collar in a layer of well-ordered ringlets. Moustaches and beards continued in favour, and varied but slightly from the style of ten years earlier.

The little maid-servant at the bottom of the page has her hair tucked away in a cap—one of the few examples of a cap of any sort worn during this period. She is fixing the extra collar on her mistress's dress. These collars were worn over the square-shaped ones, and in many contemporary portraits it is possible to see right through the outer collar of fine material to the neckline of the dress itself, which was always square in front.

Furs, gloves, masks, hoods, and veils were all important etceteras of the ladies' possessions. An interesting item which was worn from about 1630 to the end of the century was the little shoulder-cape, worn whilst the hair was being arranged and with practically any form of deshabille.

1 6 3 0—1 6 4 0 (*continued*)

The first example here is the back view of the French fashion in men's hairdressing—a bow of ribbon is here attached to the longest lock. This craze for odd bows of ribbon in the hair—ornamental perhaps, but entirely useless—remained fashionable for about thirty years, in fact until the periwig took the place of natural hair.

Black net veils were worn to protect the ladies' complexions from the harmful rays of the sun. Freckles and sunburn were considered harmful and disfiguring. To our minds this careful covering of the face, but exposure of the neck and head to the full blaze of the summer sunshine seems particularly stupid; no doubt, however, the lily-skinned beauties of the 1630's would regard our sun-tanned faces as distinctly unladylike and probably indecent.

During the winter months, still greater care was taken to prevent the skin from being roughened or exposed to the chilly winds. A hood completely encircling the face was worn, a mask covered the forehead and nose, and a chin-band was snugly arranged to conceal the jaw, so that the entire face was hidden except the mouth. Furs were worn extensively so that the ladies could snuggle under them, as we do to-day, in the teeth of an East Wind. It is questionable whether their complexions really benefited by all this tender care, but if their skins were soft and peach-like, it is, alas! impossible for us now to discover, or we might possibly be persuaded to follow in their footsteps.

The large flat-brimmed beaver or felt hat was first seen in about 1638. This style afterwards developed into the high-crowned hats of the 'forties, and the large Puritan hats worn by the Parliamentary party must have been designed from one similar to the example on the opposite page.

1640—1650

THE 'forties were turbulent and restless years; the Civil Wars breaking up the country into two distinct parties, each with their own dress, and each going to opposite extremes with their exaggerations.

The gown and suit on the opposite page show the somewhat moderated gloom of civil attire, though the man is definitely of Cavalier tendencies, judging by the bows of ribbon on his love-locks. These clothes also show the short-lived popularity of the sober dress associated with this period.

Mrs. Hutchinson, in the *Memoirs* of her husband, says : " When Puritanism grew into a faction the zealots distinguished themselves, both men and women, by several affections of habit, looks, and words, which had it been a real declension of vanity and embracing of sobriety in all those things had been most commendable in them ; but their quick forsaking of those things when they were where they would be showed that they either never took them up for conscience' sake or were corrupted by their prosperity to take up those vain things they durst not practice under persecution. Among other affected habits, few of the Puritans, whatsoever degree they were of, wore their hair long enough to cover their ears, and the ministers and many others cut it close round their heads, with so many little peaks as was ridiculous to behold—from this custom of wearing hair the name of roundhead became the scornful term given to the whole Parliament party." Colonel Hutchinson wore his hair long and curled—and, indeed, had a very fine head of hair, fanatical Puritan though he was. We may also suppose that he did not affect the ordinary Puritan garb, as his wife speaks of a handsome red velvet doublet of his.

1640—1650 (*continued*)

The Cavaliers took good care that they should not be mistaken for the opposing party, and exaggerated every fashion to the point of ridicule. The short coat, barely reaching to the waist, displayed quantities of fine shirt— and ribbons were attached to the hems of every garment. Breeches—which had assumed the proportions of a skirt by the 'fifties, were, for the most part, knee-length, and hung loose, the better to show off layers of ribbon or lace. The sides often had bows or rosettes attached—this form of ornamentation eventually resolving itself into a panel of lace or ribbon, or both, from waist to hem. The tighter form of knee-breeches was still worn, and embroidered stockings, tied up or pinned above the knee on to the breeches, were often seen, as in the figures on the top right hand of the opposite page.

Both these figures are wearing clothes more suitable to the Parliamentarians than the Royalists. Capes were extensively worn during this period, and it was also during the 'forties that the ladies' waist-line once more dropped to normal ; the exaggerated sleeves became less inflated and the neck-line lower. A curious item about the Puritan collar is worthy of note : the collar seems to have been an entirely separate affair, pinned at the throat and dropping over the shoulders, the A-shaped space in front revealing a low-necked bodice with an expanse of uncovered chest. One of these collars is worn by Elizabeth Cromwell in a contemporary miniature, and, although she wears the traditional Puritan bonnet, her hair beneath is revealed in careful ringlets.

Long aprons of finest lawn with a tiny lace edge became a part of fashionable attire during this period ; previously they had been worn only by children and domestics. A loose shoulder-cape was often worn by ladies to give additional warmth, and muffs and furs played an important part in every winter wardrobe.

1640—1650 (*continued*)

At the bottom of the opposite page will be seen a messenger boy or page in his trunk-hose. This form of nether garment was worn throughout the century by page-boys and as a Court-dress on a great many occasions.

The subdued tone and comparative simplicity of the ladies' attire at this time was probably due to the dangers a well-dressed woman was exposed to should any Parliamentarian set foot in her house. Any form of ostentation, for a few years at least, was viewed with definite disfavour.

The Cavalier light-heartedly stepped into the fray, taking an absurd delight in showing his bravery and royalty, though trammelled with feathers, lace, and love-locks. His absurd boots probably impeded him, but rather than discard one item of finery he preferred to flaunt his allegiance to the sovereign as long as the King drew breath.

In contrast a contemporary writer describes the Parliamentary party : " In high-crowned hats, collar bands, great loose coats, with long swords under them, and calves' leather boots."

The absurd fashions eventually triumphed over the more sedate fashions favoured by the Parliamentarians, and, as Mrs. Hutchinson mentions in her *Memoirs*, if any one had seen the " Roundheads " even a couple of years after their first heated demonstration of Purity—it would have been impossible to see the reason for their name.

1640—1650 (*continued*)

Ladies of Royalist inclination wore their hair in a long thick mass of curls, covering their shoulders and adorned with numerous bows of ribbon. As will be seen in the figure on the previous page, the back hair was still neatly arranged. The lady with the curls on the opposite page happens to be taken from a contemporary miniature of Cromwell's daughter, Mrs. Ireton, so that despite her Puritan tendencies her vanity was not sufficiently subdued for her to abandon and forsake her curls, in favour of the Puritan cap ; neither do her scantily-draped shoulders indicate the modesty required of Ireton's wife. Altogether, after studying the period, these Parliamentarians seem to have been a set of fanatical humbugs—with the exception, of course, of the Puritan Fathers, who were so disgusted with the vanities and immorality in England. They set themselves a rigid and austere code of life, and abandoned the country so saturated with vice, for a new World where they could practise what they believed, untrammelled by the persecution and ridicule to which sobriety and modesty had previously exposed them.

In the year 1649 Cromwell passed an Act " For the relief of felt-makers and hat-band-makers against aliens and strangers." In spite of James I's efforts, apparently, to promote the hat industry in England, foreign competition was again getting the upper hand. It is curious that Cromwell should interest himself in anything so trivial during the year of the execution of the unhappy Charles.

It is recorded in Henrietta Maria's *Memoirs* that it was she herself who originally gave the name of " Roundhead " to the Cromwellian party. Seeing for the first time this curious fashion in a Parliamentary demonstration, and being struck by one of their number, she remarked : " La ! What a handsome roundhead ! "

1650—1660

ENGLAND during the Commonwealth gives one the impression of sobriety and modesty, yet curiously enough, if we are to believe the writers—or the artists—of that day, though the latter are more conspicuous by their absence than at any other period in history, England continued to light-heartedly proceed in her extravagances and fopperies. Even without the evil example of the extravagant and reckless Court, and in spite of the crushing and bigoted influence of the Protector, the majority of the men still wore their hair long and curled, and had bows of ribbon tied to their love-locks. Ladies still wore patches on their faces to attract attention to their dimples, or other attractive features, and, what is even more extraordinary and unexpected, we learn from an entry in *Evelyn's Diary* in the year 1654 : " . . . I now observed how the women began to paint themselves, formerly a most ignominious thing and only used by prostitutes."

In the entry above this surprising piece of news we learn that he did " Visit the Mulberry Gardens, now the only place of refreshment about towne for persons of the best quality to be exceedingly cheated at ; Cromwell and his partisans having shut up and seized on Spring Gardens, which till now had been the usual rendezvous of ladies and gallants at this season." This hardly strengthens or confirms the idea of the domesticated and reformed ladies and gentlemen, virtuously renouncing the " pomps and vanities of this world," especially as John Evelyn was an excellent and worthy gentleman of a religious turn of mind.

On the opposite page will be seen the, to us laughable, habit of the dashing gallant. His absurd jacket still retains something of the tasseted skirts in the form of two-inch flaps—these flaps disappeared entirely during the 'fifties. The turned-up hat was decorated equally on both sides : a frill of lace laid round the edge of the brim and a large bunch of coloured ribbons balancing the feathers on the other side.

1650—1660 (*continued*)

Several entries from the *Diary* of Samuel Pepys in the year 1659 give us an idea of the importance attached to clothes at this period—especially those worn by this amusing humbug himself. Remembering that Pepys was the son of a tailor, and therefore as appropriately attired as the figures illustrated by Abraham Bosse, also the son of a tailor, twenty or thirty years previously, one must consider him as a definite authority on the subject.

On January 1, 1659, he writes : " This morning I rose, put on my suit with great skirts, having not lately worn any other clothes but them." (This is probably similar to the last suit on the opposite page.) However, the same suit was discarded the following month in favour of " My white suit with silver lace coat," and about the same time he wears a " Jackanapes coat with silver buttons " ; none of which sound at all Puritanical. He presents his wife with £5, to buy herself a petticoat (after spending three or four times as much on himself), and receives an unpleasant shock when she returns to him and, apparently innocently, tells him that his father has persuaded her to buy a fine cloth at twenty-six shillings a yard, and please may she have some more money as it must have some fine lace upon it ! On the following Sunday he expresses his regret that the petticoat " makes no great show," being " light coloured and lace all over silver." But he takes care that she treats this expensive garment with due care, and severely reprimands her when she leaves it untidily in the bedroom. This historian tells us that shoes were exceedingly uncomfortable when new, and he frequently records the agony of wearing a new pair of shoes. One entry describes their walk to church with his wife wearing new footwear : " My wife exceedingly troubled by a pair of new pattens and I vexed to go so slow."

1650—1660 (*continued*)

Riding-habits seem to have been exactly similar to men's suits. A lady's riding-habit described by Pepys several years later, was probably designed in a similar manner to the example on page 53. He writes : " Walking in the galleries I find the Ladies of Honour dressed in their riding garbs, with coats and doublets with deep skirts, just for all the world like mine, and buttoned their doublets up the breast, with perriwig and with hats : so that, only for a long petti-coat dragging under their men's coats, nobody could take them for women in any point whatever ; which was an odd sight, and a sight did not please me." The effeminacy of his own clothing obviously did not strike him. Probably these suits were similar to the one on page 53.

Men's heads, before the fashion for periwigs became general, were decorated and curled to ridiculous extremes. Each curl that fell over the gallant's shoulder must be adorned with a bow of ribbon—sometimes even the back curls were divided and tied. The crowns of hats were often eight or nine inches in height, and the brims received divers attentions in the complicated arrangements of ribbons, lace, feathers, and plumes.

1 6 5 0—1 6 6 0 (*continued*)

In contrast the ladies' heads must have seemed small ; curls were not worn to any great excess, unless the wearer was blessed with natural curls, the hair being dressed with merely a slight wave and rarely reaching lower than the chin. Fine jewels and pearls still adorned the head, but it was not until after the Restoration that the hair was extravagantly dressed. The back-view of the hood on the opposite page shows how it was gathered to allow the kiss-curls at the nape of the neck to be clearly seen.

It is probable that as widows were so much in evidence during this decade that the heavy weeds worn previously became an unwarrantable expense and an indication of their political inclinations. At all events, the charming little peaked black cap with the white lining became a fashionable and exceedingly attractive form of mourning. The heavy veiling was probably rejected by the Royalists as being too sombre to express their extravagant views, and too similar to the dreary uniform adopted by the Puritan fanatics.

1660—1670

WITH the arrival of Charles II into England, and the reinstallation of a Court—fresh outbursts of wild gaiety and rejoicings led the country into a whirl of thoughtless extravagance and immorality.

John Evelyn writes of the King's coronation in 1661: "Clad in the fantastig habits of the time the magnificent traine or horseback, as much as embroidery, velvet, cloth of gold and silver, and jewels, could make them and their pransing horses, proceeded through the streets strewed with flowers, houses hung with rich tapestry, windoes and balconies full of ladies."

The same spirit of intoxication seems to have continued for several years, and with it the squandering of vast sums upon clothes and articles of adornment.

Curiously enough the men far surpassed the women in their overdressing—some of the ladies looking positively sombre in contrast to the feathered, laced, and beribboned gallants. Rather charming were the little black velvet coats edged with white fur of Dutch origin, as worn by the lady in the picture on page 7. Their simplicity strikes a quaint note in contrast to the ladies' flowered and laced garments. Lace played such an important part in the clothes of the day that no lady wished to be without at least one gown "laced all over."

Pepys has great difficulty with his wife in this particular. After forbidding her to go to the extravagance of buying one of these gowns—her new one arrives covered in lace, and her old one also appears with narrow lace "all over"—she seemingly surprised at this error! Pepys also notes on August 29, 1660: "This is the first day that ever I saw my wife with black patches since we were married." Patches had, however, been introduced towards the end of Charles I's reign.

Both long coats and "jackinapes," or short waist-length coats, were worn at this period. Some of the latter type of suit were carried to ridiculous absurdity—as in the example at the bottom of the opposite page. Ribbons of several different shades were worn on the same garment, or sometimes embroidered ribbons or multi-coloured ribbons.

The collars of the suits at this time continued to be high and stiffened—the cravat being worn over the coat and entirely separate.

1660—1670 (*continued*)

In the year 1665 Evelyn (according to himself) suggests a new mode of attire after the " Eastern Fashion," which the King light-heartedly adopts for a short time. Unfortunately no examples of this type of dress remain, although both Pepys and Rugge mention it. Evelyn's records on October 18 of this year : " To Court. It being the 1st time his Majesty put himself solemnly into the Eastern Fashion of vest, changeing doublet, stiff collar, bands, and cloake, into a comely vest, after the Persian mode, with girdle or straps, and shoe-strings and garters into bouckles of which some were set with precious stones, resolving never to alter it, and to leave the French mode, which had hitherto obtained to our greate expense and reproch. Upon which divers courtiers and gentlemen gave his Majesty gold by way of wager that he would not persist in resolution." And by the 30th of that month he had himself adopted these clothes : " To London to our office, and I had on the vest and surcoat or tunic as 'twas call'd, after his Majesty had brought the whole court to it. It was a comely and manly habit, too good to hold, it being impossible for us in good earnest to leave the Monsieurs vanities long." Pepys describes the " Eastern Fashion " : " Being a long cassocke close to the body, of black cloth, and pinked with white silk under it, and a coat over it and legs ruffled with black riband like a pigeon leg."

And Rugge: "Viz. a close coat of cloth pinkt with a white taffety under . . . This in length reached the calf of the leg, and upon that a surcoat cutt at the breast, which hung loose and shorter than the vest 6 inches. The breaches of the Spanish cut, and buskins some of cloth some of leather, but of the same colour as the vest or garment."

In these descriptions we see the first appearance of the vest (or waistcoat as it eventually became) and long coat. I have searched in vain for a contemporary example of the "surcoat shorter than the vest 6 inches"; probably this was an experimental stage in its development, but the fundamentals of the eighteenth-century suit were there.

The fashion in England of wearing the skirts tucked up, tied up, and pinned up, continued in favour throughout the century, and was an excellent excuse for ladies to wear two beautiful petticoats instead of one.

The waist-line continued to move downward. Jewellery —especially pearls, were necessary accessories to any well-dressed woman. Pepys buys his wife a necklace of pearls— three rows for £80, and another at an earlier date for £4, 10s., so that apparently any price might be paid for these baubles.

1660—1670 (continued)

Periwigs became more and more prevalent, in the year 1663, Pepys has his hair cut—buys a periwig for £4, and has his own hair made into another for 25s. Ladies wore them only in riding-dress, and then over their own hair. Frequently, however, artificial curls were worn attached to the sides of the head. Hats were still large and decorated with feathers, although as the 'seventies approach the tall hat becomes less fashionable, and the large-brimmed hat with a low crown increases in favour. This hat was the forerunner of the tricorn worn throughout the eighteenth century. By about 1670 some of the hats took on a definitely three-cornered aspect.

Feminine head-dressing was somewhat severe at this period, the hair being drawn back from the face and arranged in an oval " bun " at the back—the " bun " being tied each side with ribbons, or decorated with gems or artificial flowers. Curls were worn at the side of the face resting on the shoulders, and a short-curled fringe or sometimes a row of tiny curls adorned the forehead—these were termed " Cruches."

Hats were rarely worn by the fairer sex—the hood dis-arranging the hair less, and infinitely more camouflaging should the owner wish to go abroad masked to an illicit rendezvous. With cloak, hood, mask, and fan, little or no chance of recognition was possible.

It will be noticed from the accompanying illustrations that ladies' neckwear was either décolleté in the extreme or the exact reverse—one's collar was either to one's throat or else did not begin till after the shoulders were exposed ; in either case lace or fine net must be the only material used.

Pepys mentions his " Best black cloth suit trimmed with scarlet ribbon, very neat, and my cloake lined with velvet— a new beaver, which altogether is very noble with my black silk knit canions "—canions in this case meaning the over-stockings worn loose and dropping down like a boot, and similar to the examples on the previous page. In 1668 he puts on " A New Stuff suit with a shoulder belt according to the new fashion and the bands of my vest tunique laced with silk lace of the same colour." These shoulder bands may also be observed in the drawings.

Black was an exceedingly fashionable colour ; Pepys mentions several black suits of his, and a black silk dress of his wife's " laced all over with black lace point."

1670—1680

THE period of the short coat had definitely come to an end by about the year 1668. The long-skirted type of coat once installed, remained in favour for over a century. These coats were first worn with a belt or sash tied round the waist, and a long waistcoat of varying length reaching from shoulder to the middle of the thigh, or to the bottom of the coat was specially fashionable. Breeches were often made of black velvet, contrasting with a coloured coat, and these continued to be ornamented with ribbons, lace, and fringe for several years after the installation of the skirted coat. Ornamental sword belts, or shoulder belts as they were often termed, were worn a great deal as part of the necessary civil dress. The sleeve of the coat rarely reached below the elbow, and was turned back in an elaborate cuff—cut in a variety of complicated designs. Often the waistcoat had long sleeves, and these were sometimes turned back over the cuff of the coat-sleeve. Occasionally they were worn tight nearly to the wrist, from whence the luxurious lace-frills of the shirt bunched out in a cascade of lace and silk. Ribbons were still worn at shoulder, elbow, and knee, and beautiful embroideries adorned the split skirt at the back of the coat, down the facings and the pockets. The cravat was usually tied with a small bow of ribbon—this fashion later developed into the stiff formal arrangement of scarlet ribbons.

1670—1680 (*continued*)

The periwig took on vast proportions during the 'seventies, and increased in size until about 1710—when it was supplanted by the white wig. Boots were not often worn except for riding—the fashionable form of footwear being that with a high tongue or flap reaching from four to six inches above the instep.

The gentleman on the opposite page has his " flaps " cut in an ornamental fashion, and falling down over the buckle ; these were usually lined with silk or a contrasting shade of leather. Heels were high and sometimes red. An excellent example of the type of breeches worn on the opposite page may be seen at the Victoria and Albert Museum.

Ladies' fashions definitely changed during the 'seventies. Not only the hairdressing, but practically every item altered slightly. Trains were often worn at Court, and at other times the skirts were drawn back in a somewhat formal manner giving the effect of a bustle. The fashionable bodice was very tight and low-waisted, with a tiny sleeve either pinned up or turned back well above the elbow. High collars were not so prevalent as the low neckline dropping off the shoulders at the side and forming a V in front. Flowered taffety, moire, and flowered tabby were favourite materials—floral patterns being more in use from the 'seventies onwards than previously, and a patterned material was more usual than one decorated with lace and ribbons. All these silks were exquisitely embroidered by hand, and the designs were amazingly naturalistic in manner. So beautiful were these minute posies that it seems almost incredible to us in this age of hustle and bustle that any human being could find the time and have the inexhaustible patience to cover dozens of yards of silk with almost invisible stitches.

The smocks or under-garments at this period had immense bunched and gathered sleeves—infinitely fuller than those of the bodice and always decorated with a deep frill of lace or embroidery. Several hundred illustrations would be an inadequate reference to seventeenth-century ornamentation. Unfortunately there is no opportunity for even a few examples of small details of lace and embroidery ornamentation to be inserted in these pages, but should the reader be sufficiently interested, dozens of interesting examples of the exquisite needlework executed by our industrious ancestors will be found in the Victoria and Albert Museum.

1 6 7 0 — 1 6 8 0 (*continued*)

Gloves of an elbow length were again introduced about 1670 and worn on practically every occasion. The hood and mask still played an important part in every wardrobe, and the frilled beribboned " pinner " was first seen on these shores in the late 'seventies. Muffs, furs, sunshades, tippets —more often termed " Palatines "—painted fans, velvet shoes, long gloves, and embroidered stockings were all necessary etceteras.

The complexion received more attention than hitherto. Lily-white hands were acquired by the wearing of chicken-skin gloves at night. " Plumpers " were added to sunken cheeks, these were small balls of some flexible substance, jammed into the mouth, and poked up into the cheeks to give their wearers a youthful and chubby facial contour.

Many and varied were the styles in masculine head-gear, including the flat-brimmed, low-crowned beaver similar to that at the top of the opposite page. The high-crowned style with many feathers arranged at the back was the French mode, and not worn later than about 1672. Many varieties of the tricorn were also popular, and the fashion for turning the brim right back from the face and lining the edge with ostrich feathers was extremely prevalent.

1 6 7 0—1 6 8 0 (*continued*)

When Charles II's youngest sister arrived in England in the year 1670, she brought with her in her train the famous friends of Louis XIV, Madame de Queraille. This beautiful woman wore her hair dressed in an entirely new mode —similar to that in the centre of the opposite page. The sides of the hair were curled and puffed and brushed out in a mass of small ringlets, whilst the centre parting and flatness on the top of the head remained in sharp contrast to the bunched sides ; the back hair was worn long, and drawn over the shoulders in several ringlets. Many pictures of the famous Court beauties have their hair dressed after this fashion—including Nell Gwynne.

The little lace caps were very fashionable. They were always adorned with a bow of ribbon in the front, and the hair was curled and cut so as to form a massive fringe of curls over the forehead. The back hair was drawn back and tied in a gigantic " boss " or bundle, called a choux. This was a very charming fashion, but seems to have been more in favour in France than in England. Madame Fontage wore the first top-knot ; which was named after her. From this top-knot of curls and ribbons evolved gradually the tall headdress of lace, wire and ribbons which was so essential a part of a lady's attire from the 1680's into the eighteenth century.

1680—1690

HERE is seen the amazing use of ribbon during the 'eighties; dozens of yards must have been required to tie the front of this lady's corsage, and hardly less to decorate her swain's wrists, shoulders, hat, throat, sword, and garters. The gown is made of flowered tabby and decorated with fine black net lace. The gathered frill at the feet was extremely fashionable, and so was the fringe at the hem, or a deep band of inserted lace or embroidery. Her companion is wearing a suit of black cloth, with a flowered tabby vest and gold lace at the hands. His " mouchoir " decorated with fine lace hangs gracefully from his otherwise entirely ornamental pockets—" handkerchief " was considered a vulgar word at this period !   The ribbons on his coat are scarlet, also the dozens of buttons.

The daughter of Evelyn the diarist gives such a wonderful description of the fashionable lady in her *Voyage into Maryland; or, The Ladies' Dressing-Room Unlocked*, that any other description would seem futile.   She satirically records the bare necessities a wife will demand of her poor deluded husband :

" . . . Of Point d'Espagne a rich Cornet,
Two night-Rails, and a Scarf beset
With a great Lace, a Collaret.
One black gown of Rich Silk, which odd is
Without one Colour'd, Embroider'd Bodice.
Four Petticoats for Page to hold up,
Four short ones nearer to the Crup :
Three Manteaus nor can Madam lefs
Provision here for due undrefs.
Nor demy Sultane, Spagnolet,
Nor Fringe to sweep the Mall forget :
Of under Bodice—3 neat pair
Embroidered, and of Shoos as fair :
Short under Petticoats pure fine,
Some of Japan Stuff, some of Chine.
With knee hight Galoon bottomèd,
Another quilted White and Red ;
With a broad Flanders Lace below :
Four pair of Bas de foy shot through
With silver, Diamond Buckles too,
For Garters, and as Rich for show.
Twice twelve day smocks of Holland fine,

1680—1690 *(continued)*

With cambric sleeves, rich Points joyn
(For she despises Collertine).
Twelve more for night, all Flanders lac'd,
Or else she'll think her self disgraced.
The same her Night-gown must adorn,
With two Point Waistcoats for the morn :
Of Pocket Mouchoirs hope to drain,
A dozen lac'd, a dozen plain.
Three night Gowns of rich Indian Stuff,
Four Cushion-Cloths are fcarce enough
of Point, and Flanders, nor forget
Slippers embroidered on Velvet. . . ."

Here is a glossary of some of the terms used above, with
a few of the other quaint but interesting terms in use at the
time :

Rayonne — Upper hood, pinn'd in Circle like the Sun-Beams.
Raggs — Names used for all sorts of Point Lace, etc.
Spannish paper — A beautiful red colour, ladies in Spain use
    for rouge.
Sprunkin — A narrow sleeved gown.
Sultane — A gowne trimmed with buttons or loops.
Surtout — Night Hood covering the entire dress.
Pennache — A bunch or tassel of small ribbon.
Echelles — Stomacher laced with ribbons.
Campaine — A narrow picked lace.

One must visualize the dainty gentlemen of this time
drinking chocolate, taking snuff, and nonchalantly combing
their periwigs in public :

" . . . Fops and men of wigs and snuff,
Knights of the famous Oyster Barrel Muff."

1680—1690 (continued)

Muffs were worn by all fashionable gentlemen after about 1688–89. They were immense things, and attached to their wearers' waists by a wide belt and a large ring to which they were sewn. One of these may be seen on the page opposite.

The full-skirted coats were cut with a decided " waist," somewhat lower than the natural waist-line, and pleats or gores were inserted to give extra width to the skirts. The pockets which had originally served a useful purpose were now merely a place for added ornament and embroidery— frequently even these so-called pockets were non-existent, consisting of a band of some contrasting stuff or embroidery sewn on to the coat skirts, often only a few inches from the hem of the coat, and completely out of reach of the hands. Buttons were worn in large quantities on both vest and coat, and often the sleeves were decorated with them.

Breeches became tighter, and by about 1685 had ceased to be at all ornamental—in fact, they were no longer visible beneath the long-skirted coat. Stockings were worn drawn up over the knee and gartered just below ; sometimes two garters were worn, one above the knee and one below. Buckles on shoes took the place of the earlier bow or tie, and heels were worn even higher than during the 'seventies.

Flirting gracefully over a painted fan, their ladies also supped the fashionable chocolatè or their cups of coffee. Their faces were patched, powdered, and rouged, and their hair arranged in a multitude of curls—each and every one with a different name. And piled upon their heads a variety of lace and ribbon conglomeration known as the " com- mode"—this will be dealt with later. So complicated was this " commode " that it attracted the jeering attention of every satirist and poet of the period. In her *Mundus Muliebris*, Evelyn's daughter remarks after a complicated description of head-tiring :

> " Thus face that erst near head was plac'd,
> Imagine now about the waist !

A passion for spot patterns, stripes, and plaids prevailed in ladies' clothes during the 'eighties and 'nineties, and fringe was used as an adornment to any garment. The " Echelles " or stomacher laced with ribbon was more fashionable than the plain bodice. Skirts became fuller as the period advanced towards the 'nineties, trains frequently being worn.

1680—1690 (*continued*)

No lady was seen abroad without her head dressed up in the most extraordinary manner. Patching was carried to ridiculous extremes—the mouche was often worn not only on the face but on the neck and shoulders. These patches were cut in a variety of shapes—stars, moons, etc., being the simplest and most usual forms.

One of the delightful satires of the period includes a minute description of head-tiring ; unfortunately so much of it requires translation that a complete dictionary of the period is necessary. However, a small portion of these head arrangements will be found on the following pages, with a minute glossary for those who are interested :

> " The Settee, Cupée place aright
> Frelange, Frontange, Favourite,
> Monte la haut, and Palifade,
> Sorti, Flandan (great helps to trade),
> Burgoigne, Jardiné, Cornett.
> Frilal next upper Pinner fet . . ."

Pinner — A fan-shaped, pleated frill standing up in the front of the bonnet.
Settee — The double pinner.
Cupée — A special kind of pinner.
Frelange — The bonnet and pinner together.
Frontage — Top knot.
Favourite — Locks on temple.
Monte la haut — The wire to raise the head-dress.
Palifade — A wire sustaining the hair next the first knot.
Sorti — A knot of ribbons to be seen between the pinner and the bonnet.
Flandan — A species of pinner joined to the bonnet.
Burgoigne — The frill nearest the hair.
Jardiné — The single pinner next the Burgoigne.
Cornett — The upper pinner dangling about the cheeks.

Besides all this, the Palisade, though not decorative, served its purpose as a wire frame for holding up all this absurd affair ; the entire head-dress being called a Commode —which actually was a frame of wire, covered in silk, on which the head attire could be adjusted at once upon the head. The men's periwigs imitated the ladies' hairdressing in the two " horns " or curls directly over the forehead.

1690—1700

THE bustle in its first form was introduced about 1690. The increasing tendency to bunch the skirts at the back during the 'eighties eventually resulted in a roll of padding round the back and sides of the petticoat, to give a yet wider silhouette. The bustle of the nineteenth century resembled that of the seventeenth century in many particulars : the tight-laced bodice and the frilled and ornamental petticoat was in some cases almost identical with that worn by our own mothers and grandmothers. Some of the Parisienne fashion-plates of this time might almost be those of the last century.

Ornament took on a formality similar to metal-work or iron-work, and the embroidered waistcoat worn by the ladies might almost have been a piece of armour so formal was it.

I have purposely omitted the waistcoat from the last figure on the opposite page, so that the knee-breeches may be seen. This type was first worn in the late 'eighties, and by about 1695 the fuller ones had ceased to exist. The skirt, it may be observed, was still full, with large sleeves and frills at the waist, the neck-line being brought right up to the throat and finished with a tiny band or frill. The cravat was often several yards in length, of silk, linen, or lace, and the ends always ornamented in some manner.

1690—1700 (*continued*)·

The excessive ornamentation of ladies' attire may well be noticed on the example opposite. Gold braid and embroidery played a prominent part in decoration in the 'nineties. The sleeve, it will be observed, was no longer turned back into a cuff at the elbow, but often fell loose in a bell shape over the smock sleeve. The hair was often worn loose down the back, and especially by younger women, from about 1690.

In the example of men's attire it will be noticed that his cuffs are four deep. The excess of ribbons at this period was equal if not more than in earlier periods, though after 1692 only the scarlet bow was worn at the throat, the rest of the coat decoration relying on fur, braid, and embroidery. It should here be noticed how the cravat was wound around the neck and tied, hanging over the formal arrangement of ribbons. When untied, it was sometimes slipped through a button-hole on the coat, as illustrated on the previous page.

The periwig no longer resembled the human hair, but was arranged in a mass of curls, those on the surface being cut at different lengths, to give the effect of ringlets all over. These locks were arranged in three or four separate bunches. Sometimes one mass behind and one over each shoulder, sometimes two at the back, as will be noticed on one of the previous pages—the back view of a gentleman in a black coat. The front of the wig was raised in two tufts over the temples, and the back of the head was left smooth to the nape of the neck, where the curls began.

Powder for the wig was introduced during the 'nineties, and although this method of hairdressing was not general for some years, there are many contemporary portraits of the periwig smothered in powder, and giving a greyish matted effect. A contemporary description of the youth who would be a gallant includes :

" A powder'd Wig, a Sword, a page, a chair,
Learn to take snuff, drink chocolate and swear."

1690—1700 (*continued*)

In both examples of male attire on the opposite page, the long-sleeved waistcoat may be observed beneath the enormous cuff of the coat. The cuffs were more often than not well below the elbow after 1675. The first figure shows an exaggerated form of the curls over the temples. The ornate cuffs and pockets on this coat were decorated with black fur.

In Celia Fiennes' *Through England on Horseback*, there is an interesting description worthy of record of perhaps the earliest type of bathing suit : " The ladye goes into the bath with garments made of yellow canvas, which is stiff and made large with great sleeves like a parson's gown. The water fills it up so that it's borne off that your shape is not seen, it does not cling close as other lining." She goes on to say that the gentlemen wear drawers and waistcoats of the same sort of canvas. She also mentions in the same interesting, though monotonous, volume that Canterbury was a wonderful city with many French people, whose chief industry was silk-weaving. This silk-weaving must have been that alluded to at the beginning of this book.

Muffs and furs continued in favour during the 'nineties, the muffs usually being decorated with large bows of ribbon. The furs or palatines were always fastened with jewelled tags and clasps. The fashionable colour of fur included sable, ermine, and grey. Velvet scarves were often worn over the head-dress instead of the Rayonne.

1690—1700 (*continued*)

Every curl has its fashionable position and name. There
were the Berger, Passague, Choux, Confidents, Cheve cœur,
Cruches, and Frontange. The Berger was a plain small
lock of hair turned up with a puff. The Passague was the
curled lock at the temples. Confidets were the tiny curls
near the ears. The Cheve cœur, or " heart-breakers," were
the two small curled locks at the nape of the neck. The
top drawings on the opposite page are taken from a doll—
now in the Victoria and Albert Museum—which is believed
to have been a gift to Queen Anne from a lady-in-waiting.

The head-dress (*c.* 1690) or double pinner in this instance,
is made from fine tucked lawn and is not pleated. The lace
edge is sewn on to the wire framework. Wires which originally supported the formally arranged bunches of ribbon can
still be seen between, behind, and in front of the two up-
standing frills. In this perfect contemporary example the
whole head-dress is made in one with the bonnet.

In Defoe's *Moll Flanders* we read that as a child Moll was
given " Linen to make, laces to mend and heads to dress
up," and in her endeavour to be a gentlewoman she was
given head-dresses and linen by her benefactress. Obviously
the head-dresses were a most necessary part of even ordinary
wear, for at this stage in the infamous young lady's career
she was still in an orphanage.

We also learn from the same source that a small packet of
lace stolen from a shop-counter fetched as much as £20,
which in those days (Defoe dates the book as 1683 though
it was not published until 1722) was a very great deal of
money.

1690—1700 (*continued*)

Here, then, is the rough outline of the costumes worn during the Stuart Period, from the last years of Elizabeth's reign to within two years of Queen Anne's : a hundred years packed with incident and intrigue, experiment and enterprise, yet outstanding in its social and cultural progress.

We can trace the apparently sudden change from gigantic farthingale and long stiff stomacher of Elizabeth's declining years, to the soft, high-waisted gowns so beautifully portrayed by Van Dyck, and see how this style developed by easy stages into the bustle and formal head-dressing as worn by Queen Mary II and Queen Anne. We can see how men's enormous, bombasted breeches slowly deflated, took on a variety of experimental shapes from frilled knee-breeches to the immense " Petticoat " breeches worn by Pepys and how they eventually developed into the close-fitting knee-breeches which became the standard wear of the eighteenth century. We also see how men's doublets—stiff and armorial in cut and decoration—turned by gradual stages and amusing experiment, into the long, full skirted coat which also remained in favour for well over a century ; how the waistcoat first made its appearance and how barbers and periwig makers learned to make their fortunes by exaggerating styles in hair-dressing until a natural head of hair was the most unnatural sight imaginable.

English Costume as a separate study at this time is well-nigh impossible owing to the immense variety of French and Dutch styles that were introduced. That the men followed slavishly in the French fashions was noted by Evelyn in 1665, and the ladies were certainly no less influenced especially when French fashion plates appeared in printed form a few years later.

New styles during the second half, at least, of the seventeenth century, became a competitive amusement amongst all those who could afford to indulge their taste in the latest thing in foreign fashion.